THANK HEAVEN FOR COFFEE (AND OTHER LITTLE PLEASURES)

BARBOUR
PUBLISHING

MORNING EXHILARATION!

The morning cup of coffee has an exhilaration about it which the cheering influence of the afternoon or evening cup of tea cannot be expected to reproduce.

—Oliver Wendell Holmes Sr.

DAY 2

BE BLESSED

May there always be work for your hands to do; may your purse always hold a coin or two. May the sun always shine on your windowpane; may a rainbow be certain to follow each rain. May the hand of a friend always be near you; may God fill your heart with gladness to cheer you.

—IRISH BLESSING

THE DRINK OF TURKS

The Turks have a drink of black colour. . . .
They swallow it hot as it comes from the
fire and they drink it in the long draughts,
not at dinner time, but as a kind of dainty and
sipped slowly while talking with one's friends.
One cannot find any meetings among
them where they drink it not. . . .

—ITALIAN EXPLORER

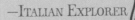

DAY 4

RICHES IN GLORY

*But my God shall supply all your
need according to his riches
in glory by Christ Jesus.*

—PHILIPPIANS 4:19 KJV

COFFEE IS BEST SERVED. . .

. . .black

. . .or with cream

. . .or with sugar

. . .or flavored with vanilla, chocolate, hazelnut, peppermint, spice, etc.

. . .or with dessert

. . .or with breakfast

. . .or with a smile

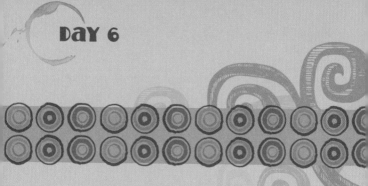

DAY 6

WHAT WE LOVE

We are shaped and fashioned
by what we love.

—JOHANN WOLFGANG VON GOETHE

SLEEP

A morning without coffee feels like sleep,
but a night with it sleep eludes.

—UNKNOWN

DAY 8

THE BEST TIME OF DAY FOR COFFEE IS. . .

. . .breakfast for a jump start
. . .mid-morning for inspiration
. . .lunch for good measure
. . .mid-afternoon for a restart
. . .dinner for a conversation starter
. . .evening for a happy ending

DESIRES OF YOUR HEART

Delight yourself in the LORD and he will give you the desires of your heart.

—PSALM 37:4 NIV

A PRICELESS GIFT

Every day we live is a priceless gift of God,
loaded with possibilities to learn
something new, to gain fresh insights
into His great truths.

—DALE EVANS ROGERS

THE COIN OF LIFE

Time is the coin of your life. It is the only coin you have, and only you can determine how it will be spent. Be careful lest you let other people spend it for you.

—CARL SANDBURG

WHAT IS REAL COFFEE?

A cup of coffee—real coffee—home-browned, home ground, home made, that comes to you dark as a hazel-eye, but changes to a golden bronze as you temper it with cream that never cheated, but was real cream from its birth, thick, tenderly yellow, perfectly sweet, neither lumpy nor frothing on the Java: such a cup of coffee is a match for twenty blue devils and will exorcise them all.

—HENRY WARD BEECHER

A WISE USE OF TIME

Nothing is a waste of time if you
use the experience wisely.

—RODIN

EVERY MORNING

Your first words every morning should be,
here I am, send me.

—JOHN MASON

THE FIRST OF MORNING

The men who have done the most for God in
this world have been early on their knees.
He who fritters away the early morning,
its opportunity and freshness, in other
pursuits than seeking God will make poor
headway seeking Him the rest of the day.
If God is not first in our thoughts and efforts
in the morning, He will be in the last
place the remainder of the day.

—E. M. BOUNDS

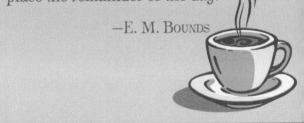

SNOWFLAKE

The wonder of a single snowflake outweighs
the wisdom of a million meteorologists.

—SIR FRANCIS BACON

UNFATHOMABLE WONDERS

He performs wonders that cannot be fathomed, miracles that cannot be counted.

—JOB 5:9 NIV

SUAVE MOLECULES

Coffee detracts nothing from your intellect; on the contrary, your stomach is freed by it and no longer distresses your brain; it will not hamper your mind with troubles but give freedom to its working. Suave molecules of Mocha stir up your blood, without causing excessive heat; the organ of thought receives from it a feeling of sympathy; work becomes easier and you sit down without distress.

—PRINCE TALLEYRAND

OUR FUTURE

We are made wise not by the recollection of our past, but by the responsibility for our future.

—GEORGE BERNARD SHAW

CAFÉ MOCHA

Mix 1 ounce chocolate syrup and 1 shot espresso. Fill the remainder of the coffee mug with steamed milk. Garnish with whipped cream and chocolate sprinkles.

TODAY IS A GIFT

Yesterday is history. Tomorrow is a mystery.
And today? Today is a gift.
That's why we call it the present.

—BABATUNDE OLATUNJI

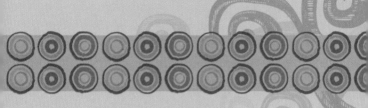

A STRONG DRINK OF CHOICE

Coffee—a strong drink of choice—so strong
that certain religious sectors choose to
ban their members from partaking.
Even Grandma preaches that it will curl
the toes and put hair on the chest.

Give Strong Drink

Give strong drink unto him that is ready to perish, and wine unto those that be of heavy hearts. Let him drink, and forget his poverty, and remember his misery no more.

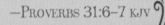

—Proverbs 31:6–7 kjv

QUIET AND COMFORT

If we have not quiet in our minds,
outward comfort will do no more for us
than a glass slipper on a gouty foot.

—JOHN BUNYAN

CREATE TIME

Create some time for daily spiritual renewal.
Relax in your favorite chair with hot tea
(or coffee), your Bible, a devotional, and a
simple treat. Enjoy!

—MARY & MARTHA

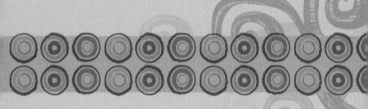

LOOK FOR TRUTH

If you look for truth, you may find comfort in
the end; if you look for comfort you will not
get either comfort or truth. . . .

—C. S. Lewis

ETERNAL BLESSINGS

A man may lose the good things of this life against his will; but if he loses the eternal blessings, he does so with his own consent.

—Augustine

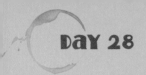

Inspire

Treat people as if they were what they ought
to be and you help them to become
what they are capable of being.

—Johann Wolfgang von Goethe

BEETHOVEN'S COFFEE

It is said that Ludwig van Beethoven was very particular about his coffee, counting out exactly sixty beans to brew just one cup. Perhaps his caffeine high was what inspired his musical masterpieces.

COFFEE FUDGE SAUCE

2 tablespoons instant coffee granules
½ cup vanilla-flavored liquid coffee creamer
1 cup marshmallow creme
4 ounces semisweet chocolate chips

In saucepan, heat coffee and creamer over low heat until granules dissolve. Add marshmallow creme and chocolate chips; stir until mixture is smooth.

THE EYES OF A CHILD

Seek the wisdom of the ages, but look
at the world through the eyes of a child.

—RON WILD

LAUGHTER

I believe laughter is like a needle
and thread. Deftly used, it can patch
up just about everything.

—BARBARA JOHNSON

NO MORE THIRST

*Whosoever drinketh of the water that
I shall give him shall never thirst.*

—JOHN 4:14 KJV

A SilveR LiNiNG

The inner side of every cloud is bright
and shining; I therefore turn my clouds
about and always wear them inside
out to show the lining.

—ELLEN THORNCROFT FOWLER

TRUE FEELINGS

Never apologize for showing feeling.
When you do so, you apologize for the truth.

—Benjamin Disraeli

sweet as love

Good coffee is black as sin, pure as the angels, strong as death, and sweet as love.

—CREOLE PROVERB

FRUIT OF LOVE

Love is a fruit in season at all times,
and within the reach of every hand.

—MOTHER TERESA

DAY 38

A CUPFUL OF LOVE

God has poured out his love into our hearts.
—ROMANS 5:5 NIV

Since we have been so loved, let us not
neglect sharing that love with others even in
the simple offering of a cup of joe.

Honey-Nut Latte

1 ounce hazelnut syrup
1 ounce honey
1 to 2 ounces hot espresso
Steamed milk
Whipped topping
Honey to taste
Nuts, finely chopped

In large mug, mix hazelnut syrup and honey with espresso; stir until honey dissolves. Fill mug with steamed milk. Garnish with whipped topping, honey, and nuts.

DAY 40

WE ARE LOVED

The greatest happiness of life is the conviction that we are loved—loved for ourselves, or rather, loved in spite of ourselves.

—Victor Hugo

HEARTFELT

The best and most beautiful things in the world cannot be seen or even touched. They must be felt with the heart.

—HELEN KELLER

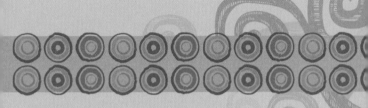

BEST PLACE TO GROW

We find comfort among those who agree with
us—growth among those who don't.

—FRANK A. CLARK

A SWEET OFFERING

No coffee can be good in the mouth that does not first send a sweet offering of odor to the nostrils.

—HENRY WARD BEECHER

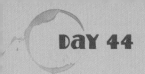
FRAGRANT OFFERING

[The gifts you sent] are a fragrant offering,
an acceptable sacrifice, pleasing to God.

—PHILIPPIANS 4:18 NIV

Live and Love

We want to live forever for the same reason that we want to live tomorrow. Why do we want to live tomorrow? It is because there is someone who loves you, and whom you want to see tomorrow, and be with, and love back.

—Henry Drummond

ADD a SPeCiaL TOUCH

Consider adding something to your coffee grounds in the basket before brewing—a spice like ground cinnamon, a coarsely ground vanilla bean, brown sugar, cocoa, pecan meal, citrus zest. . . .

THE SOWER REAPS

He who sows courtesy reaps friendship.

—St. Basil

DAY 48

PEARL OF GREAT PRICE

Contentment is a pearl of great price,
and whoever procures it at the expense
of ten thousand desires makes a wise
and happy choice.

—JOHN PIPER

DAILY GIFT

He who gives you the day will also give
you the things necessary for the day.

—GREGORY OF NYSSA

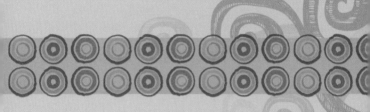

A Life Staple

Coffee played a big role in our life.
The first thing you did in the morning
was put on water, and the last thing you
did at night was take off the pot.

—PAUL PRUDHOMME, QUOTED BY JOHN DEMERS,
*THE COMMUNITY KITCHEN'S COMPLETE
GUIDE TO GOURMET COFFEE*

COFFEE BREAK

Take a coffee break for no particular
reason and invite a friend. Serve the
coffee in your collectible mugs along
with a delightful dessert.

OLD FRIENDS

The best mirror is an old friend.

—GEORGE HERBERT

FRIENDS REMEMBERED

I count myself in nothing else so happy as in
a soul rememb'ring my good friends.

—WILLIAM SHAKESPEARE

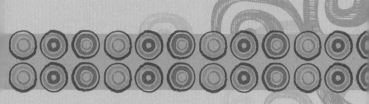

FRIEND OF THE KING

He who loves a pure heart and whose speech is gracious will have the king for his friend.

—PROVERBS 22:11 NIV

A FRIEND TO SELF

Friendship with oneself is all-important
because without it one cannot be friends
with anyone else in the world.

—ELEANOR ROOSEVELT

DAY 56

HOPE OF JOY

There is no hope of joy
except in human relations.

—Antoine de Saint-Exupéry

MY BEST

My best friend is the one who
brings out the best in me.

—HENRY FORD

DAY 58

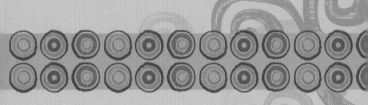

BRING ON THE SNOW

Advice is like snow; the softer it falls,
the longer it dwells upon, and the
deeper it sinks into the mind.

—SAMUEL TAYLOR COLERIDGE

TIRAMISU

24 ladyfinger cookies
1 tablespoon sugar
2 tablespoons instant coffee granules
1 cup boiling water
2 (8 ounce) packages cream cheese, softened
½ cup sugar
2 cups whipped topping
1 teaspoon unsweetened cocoa powder

Lay 12 cookies in bottom of 9x13 pan. Dissolve 1 tablespoon sugar and coffee in boiling water. Reserve half and brush rest of mixture onto cookies in pan. Beat together cream cheese and ½ cup sugar; fold in whipped topping. Spread half the mixture over cookies. Layer on 12 cookies brushed with rest of coffee. Top with remaining cheese mixture and sprinkle with cocoa. Refrigerate overnight.

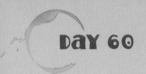

DAY 60

CAFFEINE FIX

I don't have a problem with caffeine.
I have a problem without caffeine!

—UNKNOWN

BEST A NEIGHBOR NEARBY

Do not forsake your friend and the friend of your father, and do not go to your brother's house when disaster strikes you—better a neighbor nearby than a brother far away.

—PROVERBS 27:10 NIV

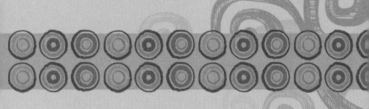

Friends Undeserved

I no doubt deserved my enemies,
but I don't believe I deserved my friends.

—Walt Whitman

HOW TO BE A FRIEND

Have a heart that never hardens,
and a temper that never tires,
and a touch that never hurts.

—CHARLES DICKENS

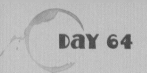

LET THERE BE LAUGHTER

In the sweetness of friendship let there be laughter, for in the dew of the little things the heart finds its morning and is refreshed.

—JAMES ALLEN

THIS DAY

My God, I give You this day.
I offer You, now,
all of the good that I shall do
and I promise to accept,
for love of You,
all of the difficulty that I shall meet.
Help me to conduct myself
during this day
in a manner pleasing to You.
Amen.

—ST. FRANCIS DE SALES

Bitter Be Gone

If you should ever encounter a cup of coffee too bitter to enjoy, add a pinch of salt and be amazed at how it mellows out the flavor into something you'll enjoy drinking.

A GOOD NAME

*A good name is more desirable than
great riches; to be esteemed is
better than silver or gold.*

—Proverbs 22:1 NIV

UNIVERSAL ESTEEM

There is no beverage which is held in more universal esteem than good coffee.

—ELIZA ACTON

POSSiBiLiTiES!

Ah! dear friend, you little know the
possibilities which are in you.

—CHARLES H. SPURGEON

FRIENDSHIP DIVINE

The most I can do for my friend is simply to be his friend. I have no wealth to bestow on him. If he knows that I am happy in loving him, he will want no other reward. Is not friendship divine in this?

—HENRY DAVID THOREAU

MOCHA DROPS

2 cups semisweet chocolate
  chips, divided
2 tablespoons instant
  coffee granules
2 teaspoons boiling water
½ cup butter, softened
½ cup white sugar
½ cup brown sugar, packed

1 egg
1¼ cups flour
¾ teaspoon baking
  soda
½ teaspoon salt
½ cup walnuts,
  chopped

Preheat oven to 350 degrees. Melt ½ cup chips
until smooth. Set aside. Dissolve coffee in
boiling water. In large bowl, blend butter,
sugars, and coffee; add egg and melted
chocolate. In separate bowl, combine dry
ingredients; gradually add to batter. Stir in
remaining chips and walnuts. Form small
balls and place on ungreased baking
sheets. Bake 10 to 12 minutes.

JUST LAUGH!

If I were given the opportunity to
present a gift to the next generation,
it would be the ability for each individual
to learn to laugh at himself.

—CHARLES SCHULZ

THE DELIGHTFUL PRESENCE

Few delights can equal the mere presence
of one whom we utterly trust.

—GEORGE MACDONALD

I Have Called You Friends

*I no longer call you servants, because a
servant does not know his master's business.
Instead, I have called you friends,
for everything that I learned from my Father
I have made known to you.*

—JOHN 15:15 NIV

THE PIÈCE DE RÉSISTANCE

Coffee is the crowning of a grand dinner. . .
the *pièce de résistance*. . . .

—LAFCADIO HEARN, *LA CUISINE CREOLE*,
19TH-CENTURY COOKBOOK

DAY 76

WIDE AWAKE

Learning sleeps and snores in libraries,
but wisdom is everywhere, wide awake, on tiptoe.

—JOSH BILLINGS

SiMPliCitY IS. . .

Simplicity is the character of the spring
of life, costliness becomes its autumn;
but a neatness and purity, like that of
the Snowdrop or Lily of the Valley, is the
peculiar fascination of beauty, to which
it lends enchantment, and gives what
amiability is to the mind.

—Henry Wadsworth Longfellow

DaY 78

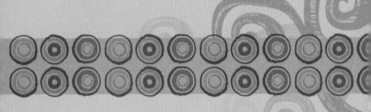

sweet Desire

The desire accomplished is sweet to the soul.

—Proverbs 13:19 kjv

A JOYFUL ENDING

Thou shalt ever joy at eventide
if you spend the day fruitfully.

—THOMAS À KEMPIS

THE JOY OF LONGING AND WISHING

After a time, you may find that
"having" is not so pleasing a thing,
after all, as "wanting." It is not logical,
but it is often true.

—SPOCK, "AMOK TIME," STARDATE 3372.7

sleeplessness

Conscience keeps more people
awake than coffee.

—Unknown

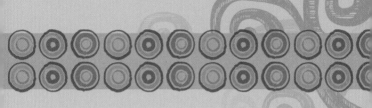

COCOA COFFEE

Divide one envelope of hot chocolate mix between two mugs of hot coffee. Top with some whipped cream for added enjoyment.

A LOYAL FRIEND

A loyal friend laughs at your jokes when
they're not so good and sympathizes with
your problems when they're not so bad.

—ARNOLD H. GLASGOW

EVERYTHING IS GOOD

*For everything God created is good,
and nothing is to be rejected if it
is received with thanksgiving,*

—1 TIMOTHY 4:4 NIV

FOR LITTLE THINGS

Thank You, God, for little things
that often come our way—
The things we take for granted
but don't mention when we pray—
The unexpected courtesy,
the thoughtful, kindly deed—
A hand reached out to help us
in the time of sudden need—
Oh, make us more aware, dear God,
of little daily graces
That come to us with "sweet surprise"
from never-dreamed-of places.

—HELEN STEINER RICE

COFFEE GROWS ON TREES

The coffee tree (or shrub) will reach maturity in about five years. And one year's worth of bean (or berry) harvest per tree only equals about a pound of roasted coffee for choice brewing.

Molasses and Cream

1½ cups (12 ounces) hot coffee
1 teaspoon molasses
⅛ cup light cream

Combine coffee and molasses in a large mug; stir until molasses dissolves. Add cream and serve.

—MARY & MARTHA

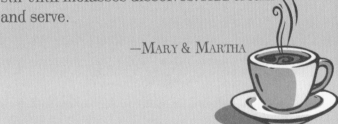

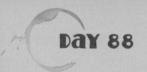

SCATTER JOY

There is no beautifier of complexion,
or form, or behavior, like the wish
to scatter joy.

—RALPH WALDO EMERSON

THE TWO WINGS

Purity and simplicity are the two wings
with which man soars above the earth
and all temporary nature.

—THOMAS À KEMPIS

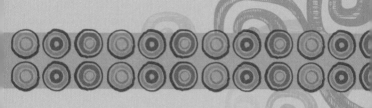

innocence

Hold fast to simplicity of heart
and innocence. Yes, be as babes who
do not know the wickedness that
destroys grown people's lives.

—Shepherd of Hermas

Be an Inspiration

He has achieved success who has loved much, laughed often, and been an inspiration to little children.

—Unknown

THANKS REMINDER

Make a list of all the things for which you're thankful. Write it on fancy stationery and display it on the refrigerator where you'll see it often—a daily reminder of everything that's good in your life.

—MARY & MARTHA

THANKS FOR ALL

We ought to give thanks for all fortune:
if it is good, because it is good, if bad,
because it works in us patience, humility,
and the contempt of this world and
the hope of our eternal country.

—C. S. LEWIS

A Banned Substance?

The International Olympic Committee has a list of prohibited substances that until 2004 included caffeine. About five cups of coffee could put an athlete over the twelve micrograms of caffeine allowed and ban them from participation in the Olympic Games. Though no longer banned, excessive caffeine use is still monitored by the committee.

JOY TO THE HEART

*A cheerful look brings joy to the heart,
and good news gives health to the bones.*

—PROVERBS 15:30 NIV

HARMLESS CHEER

I feel an earnest and humble desire,
and shall till I die, to increase the
stock of harmless cheerfulness.

—CHARLES DICKENS

THE KEY TO THE HEART

How many undervalue the power of
simplicity! But it is the real key to the heart.

—HENRY WADSWORTH LONGFELLOW

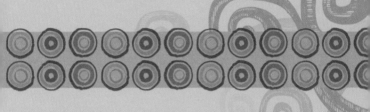

Nearest and Dearest

The best things in life are nearest:
Breath in your nostrils, light in your eyes,
flowers at your feet, duties at your hand,
the path of right just before you.

—Robert Louis Stevenson

GLORY

Lord, make me see Your glory in every place.

—MICHELANGELO

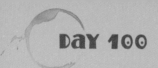

SIMPLIFY

Life is frittered away by detail. . . .
Simplify, simplify.

—HENRY DAVID THOREAU

SIMPLY LIVE

Live simply that others might simply live.

—ELIZABETH SEATON

MUSIC NIGHT

Make one evening a week music night at your home. Turn off the TV and let each family member make a musical selection for everyone to enjoy. Savor a cup of coffee, or cocoa for the kids, while you listen.

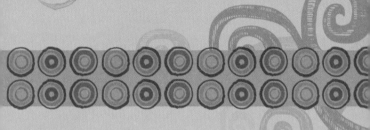

TREASURES OF HOME

With Pomp, Power & Glory the world beckons
  vainly,
In chase of such vanities why should I roam?
While Peace & Content bless my little
  thatched cottage,
And warm my own hearth with the Treasures
  of Home.

—Beatrix Potter

DRINK in PEACE

A fig for partridges and quails,
Ye dainties I know nothing of ye;
But on the highest mount in Wales
Would choose in peace to drink my coffee.

—JONATHAN SWIFT

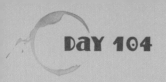

ECHoeS

Kind words can be short and easy to speak,
but their echoes are truly endless.

—MOTHER TERESA

GLORIOUS WORDS

These glorious things—words—are man's right
alone. . . . Without words we should know no
more of each other's hearts and thoughts than
the dog knows of his fellow dog. . .for, if you
will consider, you always think to yourself in
words, though you do not speak them aloud;
and without them all our thoughts would be
mere blind longings, feelings which we could
not understand ourselves.

—CHARLES KINGSLEY

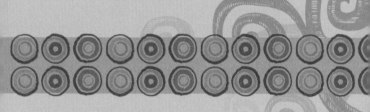

TOO MANY WONDERS

Many, O LORD my God, are the wonders you have done. The things you planned for us no one can recount to you; were I to speak and tell of them, they would be too many to declare.

—PSALM 40:5 NIV

TIMELESS LIVING

To live is so startling it leaves
little time for anything else.

—EMILY DICKINSON

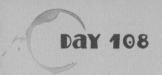

DAY 108

THE ORDINARY ARTS

The ordinary arts we practice every day at home are of more importance to the soul than their simplicity might suggest.

—Thomas More

ORANGE-CHOCOLATE COFFEE

1 cup hot strong coffee
1 cup hot chocolate
2 orange slices
Whipped topping
Dash of cinnamon

Blend coffee with hot chocolate. Place
1 orange slice into each of 2 cups. Pour
coffee mixture into cups and top with
whipped topping and cinnamon.

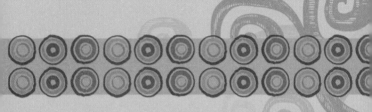

THE COFFEE CANTATA

Around 1732, Johann Sebastian Bach wrote *The Coffee Cantata* about an unmarried daughter's love for coffee. Her old-fashioned German father threatens she'll remain unmarried if she doesn't give up the java bean. She relents but adds that she'll put in the marriage contract that she be allowed three cups a day.

SHARED JOY

You can read Kant by yourself if
you wanted to; but you must share
a joke with someone else.

—ROBERT LOUIS STEVENSON

DOUBLE JOY

Shared joy is double-joy and
shared sorrow is half-sorrow.

—SWEDISH PROVERB

ENJOY THIS DAY!

Go and enjoy choice food and sweet drinks, and send some to those who have nothing prepared. This day is sacred to our Lord. Do not grieve, for the joy of the Lord is your strength.

—NEHEMIAH 8:10 NIV

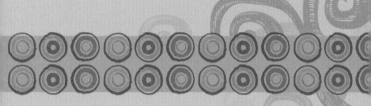

Caramel Chocolate Cappuccino

1 cup hot water
¾ cup milk
2 tablespoons chocolate syrup
3 tablespoons caramel syrup
1 tablespoon instant coffee granules

Place all ingredients in microwave-safe bowl and microwave on high for 3 minutes or until hot. Stir and pour into mugs. Serve immediately.

THE SIMPLE WORLD

The world could not exist if it were not simple. This ground has been filled a thousand years, yet its powers remain ever the same; a little rain, a little sun, and each spring it grows green again.

—JOHANN WOLFGANG VON GOETHE

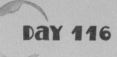

FOR THE BERRIES

We affectionately call our coffee source "beans," but the technical plant term would be "berries."

INTENSE SIMPLICITIES

Out of intense complexities
intense simplicities emerge.

—SIR WINSTON CHURCHILL

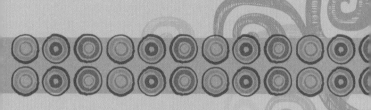

HIGHEST ASPIRATIONS

Far away there in the sunshine are my highest aspirations. I may not reach them, but I can look up and see their beauty, believe in them, and follow them where they lead.

—Louisa May Alcott

ONE CHANCE

I shall pass through this world but once.
Any good thing therefore that I can do,
or any kindness that I can show to any
human being, let me do it now. Let me not
defer it or neglect it, for I shall not
pass this way again.

—HENRY DRUMMOND

THE SMALL THINGS

Take time in your day to be inspired by
something small—the scent of a flower from
your garden, a hug from a child, an "I love
you" from your spouse. . . . Then thank God
for the little things in life.

—MARY & MARTHA

Rejoice!

*This is the day the LORD has made;
let us rejoice and be glad in it.*

—PSALM 118:24 NIV

KINDNESS

Let no one ever come to you without
leaving better and happier. Be the living
expression of God's kindness:
kindness in your face, kindness in your eyes,
kindness in your smile.

—MOTHER TERESA

COFFEE HOUSES

The first known European house of coffee opened in Venice in 1683, though coffee had been available as early as 1608 in Europe for the aristocrats.

THE HUMAN CONNECTION

No soul is desolate as long as
there is a human being for whom
it can feel trust and reverence.

—GEORGE ELIOT

REKiNDLED

At times our own light goes out and is
rekindled by a spark from another person.
Each of us has cause to think with deep
gratitude of those who have lighted the
flame within us.

—ALBERT SCHWEITZER

Eating and Drinking

Without the assistance of eating
and drinking, the most sparkling
wit would be as heavy as a bad soufflé,
and the brightest talent as dull as
a looking glass on a foggy day.

—ALEXIS SOYER, *THE MODERN HOUSEWIFE*

RED-EYE GRAVY WITH HAM

1 tablespoon butter
6 slices precooked ham at least ¼-inch thick
1 teaspoon brown sugar
½ cup brewed coffee

Melt butter in a skillet. Cook each side of ham 2 minutes. Sprinkle sugar over ham, then pour in the coffee. Cover and simmer over low heat 5 to 8 minutes.

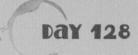

WAIT UPON GOD

In the rush and noise of life, as you have intervals, step home within yourselves and be still. Wait upon God, and feel His good presence; this will carry you evenly through your day's business.

—WILLIAM PENN

Patience

Patience with others is Love.
Patience with self is Hope.
Patience with God is Faith.

—ADEL BESTAVROS

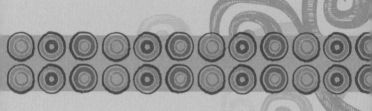

THE WONDER OF MOTHERS

Mothers are those wonderful people
who can get up in the morning
before the smell of coffee.

—UNKNOWN

TEACH THE CHILDREN

*Teach (God's words) to your children,
talking about them when you sit at home
and when you walk along the road,
when you lie down and when you get up.*

—DEUTERONOMY 11:19 NIV

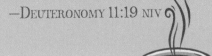

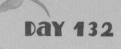

BLOOM ON THE FRUIT

Obedience is the fruit of the faith;
patience, the bloom on the fruit.

—CHRISTINA ROSSETTI

ON THE BRIGHT SIDE

I learned to look more on the bright side of
my condition, and less upon the dark side,
and to consider what I enjoyed, rather than
what I wanted; and this gave me sometimes
such secret comforts, that I cannot express
them; and which I take notice here, to put
those discontented people in mind of it,
who cannot enjoy comfortably what God
has given them, because they see and covet
something that He has not given them.
All our discontents about what we want
appeared to me to spring from the want of
thankfulness for what we have.

—DANIEL DEFOE, *ROBINSON CRUSOE*

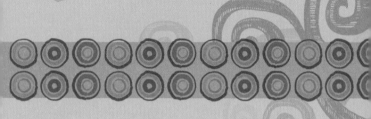

LORD, HELP US!

Lord, when we are wrong, make us
willing to change. And when we are right,
make us easy to live with.

—PETER MARSHALL

A GENERAL COMMOTION

This coffee falls into your stomach, and straightway there is a general commotion. Ideas begin to move like the battalions of the Grand Army of the battlefield, and the battle takes place.

—HONORÉ DE BALZAC, "THE PLEASURES AND PAINS OF COFFEE"

Chocolate Hazelnut Coffee

¾ cup hot water
¼ cup hot milk
2 teaspoons hazelnut-flavored instant coffee
granules
1 teaspoon cocoa
1 tablespoon dark brown sugar
1 tablespoon whipped topping

Stir together all ingredients except whipped
topping. Pour into mugs. Top with whipped
topping and serve immediately.

STAY YOUNG

You'll always stay young if you live
honestly, eat slowly, sleep sufficiently,
work industriously, and worship faithfully.

—Unknown

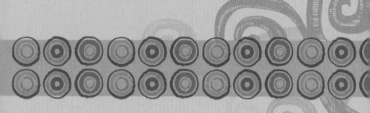

STOOD THE TEST

Blessed is the man who perseveres under trial, because when he has stood the test, he will receive the crown of life. . . .

—JAMES 1:12 NIV

REALIZE THE LOVE

Some people are led through their blessings
to realize the love of their heavenly Father.

—CHARLES ALLEN

DAILY BLESSINGS

The goodness of God is the drive behind all
the blessings He daily bestows upon us.

—A. W. TOZER

Java

The first main source of coffee beans for worldwide shipment in the 1800s came from the island of Java in Indonesia, thus giving the cup of brew the nickname of "java."

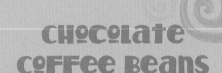

CHOCOLATE
COFFEE BEANS

Melt about ½ cup dark chocolate bits,
stirring until smooth. Then add about
⅓ cup whole coffee beans. Spread the
beans out onto waxed paper so that none
touch, and let them dry. Enjoy!

Lessons in Love

Is life not full of opportunities for learning love? Every man and woman every day has a thousand of them. The world is not a playground; it is a schoolroom. Life is not a holiday, but an education. And the one eternal lesson for us all is how better we can love.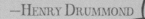

—HENRY DRUMMOND

wait Patiently

*But if we hope for what we do not yet have,
we wait for it patiently.*

—ROMANS 8:25 NIV

A MaGiCal EFFect

Patience and perseverance have a magical effect before which difficulties disappear and obstacles vanish.

—JOHN QUINCY ADAMS

PROTECTION

Patience serves as a protection against wrongs as clothes do against cold. For if you put on more clothes as the cold increases, it will have no power to hurt you. So in like manner you must grow in patience when you meet with great wrongs, and they will be powerless to vex your mind.

—LEONARDO DA VINCI

A State of Mind

Happiness is not a possession to be prized,
it is a quality of thought, a state of mind.

—DAPHNE DU MAURIER

A Manner of Traveling

Happiness is not a destination; it is a manner of traveling. Happiness is not an end in itself. It is a by-product of working, playing, loving, and living.

—Dr. Haim Ginott

THE WITTY DRINKER

The coffee is prepared in such a way that
it makes those who drink it witty: at least
there is not a single soul who, on quitting the
house, does not believe himself four times
wittier that when he entered it.

—CHARLES DE SECONDAT MONTESQUIEU

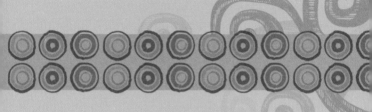

catch it!

The Constitution only gives people
the right to pursue happiness.
You have to catch it yourself.

—BENJAMIN FRANKLIN

A MERRY HEART

*He that is of a merry heart
hath a continual feast.*

—Proverbs 15:15 KJV

Coffee and Candles

Create a welcoming atmosphere in your home by placing an aromatic candle—vanilla is a good choice—in a bowl or jar. Fill the space around the candle with whole coffee beans up to an inch from the top of the candle.

SYMPHONY OF LIFE

To live content with small means; to seek
elegance rather than luxury, and refinement
rather than fashion; to be worthy,
not respectable, and wealthy, not rich;
to listen to stars and birds, babes and sages,
with open heart; to study hard;
to think quietly, act frankly, talk gently,
await occasions, hurry never; in a word, to
let the spiritual, unbidden, and unconscious
grow up through the common—this is my
symphony.

—WILLIAM HENRY CHANNING

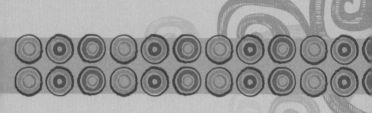

INDEPENDENCE OF SOLITUDE

It is easy in the world to live after the world's opinion; it is easy to live in solitude after our own; but the great man is he who in the midst of the crowds keeps with perfect sweetness the independence of solitude.

—RALPH WALDO EMERSON

DESTINY ACHIEVED

Destiny is not a matter of chance,
it is a matter of choice; it is not a thing to
be waited for, it is a thing to be achieved.

—WILLIAM JENNINGS BRYAN

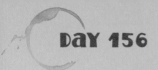

CHOICE BEVERAGE

Choicest Mocha coffee (served) in tiny cups
of egg-shell porcelain, hot, strong,
and fragrant, poured out in saucers of
gold and silver. . .to the grand dames,
who fluttered their fans with many grimaces,
bending their piquant faces. . .over the
new and streaming beverage.

—ISAAC D'ISRAELI

Cappuccino Cake

1 prepared sponge cake
2 teaspoons unflavored gelatin
1 cup boiling coffee
1 cup sweetened condensed milk
Whipped topping
Cocoa

Place the sponge cake inside a pan the same size as the cake. Dissolve the gelatin in the boiling coffee. Blend condensed milk into the coffee and pour the mixture over the sponge cake. Refrigerate at least 3 hours or until set. Top with whipped topping and a sprinkling of cocoa.

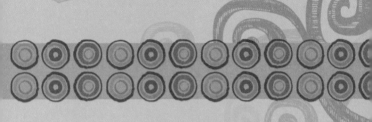

WISDOM

Wisdom is supreme; therefore get wisdom.
Though it cost all you have, get understanding.

—Proverbs 4:7 NIV

ARt oF CoFFee

As with art 'tis prepared,
so one should drink it with art.

—ARABIAN PROVERB

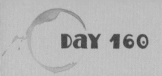

THE ART OF SIMPLICITY

The art of art, the glory of expression,
and the sunshine of the light
of letters is simplicity.

—WALT WHITMAN

ART IS. . .

Art is a collaboration between God and the artist, and the less the artist does the better.

—ANDRÉ GIDE

THE SENSE OF
THE BEAUTIFUL

A man should hear a little music, read a little poetry, and see a fine picture every day of his life, in order that worldly cares may not obliterate the sense of the beautiful which God has implanted in the human soul.

—JOHANN WOLFGANG VON GOETHE

No More Tea

During the War of 1812, when the supply of tea was cut off, America's affection for coffee was given a chance to grow, and grow, and grow.

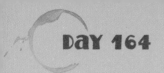
HEART BURNING

A joyful heart is the inevitable result
of a heart burning with love.

—MOTHER TERESA

WHITE CHOCOLATE COFFEE

3 ounces white chocolate, grated
2 cups whole milk
2 cups hot brewed coffee
Whipped topping (optional)

Place grated white chocolate and milk in a microwave-safe bowl and heat for 2 minutes; stir until mixture is smooth and chocolate is melted completely. Stir in coffee. Serve in large mugs and top with whipped topping if desired. Yield: 4 servings.

—MARY & MARTHA

Passionate Attention

In solitude we give passionate attention
to our lives, to our memories,
to the details around us.

—Virginia Woolf

DEVOTED FRIENDS

*A despairing man should have
the devotion of his friends.*

—JOB 6:14 NIV

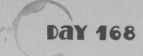

THanKS FoR FRienDS

Dear Lord, I thank You for my friends.
A true friend sees me and not my faults,
just like You do.

SHARE THE JOY AND GRIEF

It [friendship] redoubleth joy,
and cutteth griefs in halves.

—SIR FRANCIS BACON

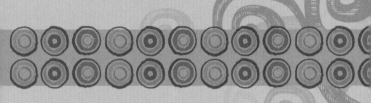

COFFEE AND CREAM

Best friends complement each other as
one is the coffee and one is the cream.

A WHOLE PERSON

No man is the whole of himself;
his friends are the rest of him.

—HARRY EMERSON

ICED VANILLA COFFEE

⅓ cup sugar
4 cups strong brewed coffee
½ teaspoon vanilla
½ cup half-and-half

Dissolve sugar in hot coffee, then add vanilla. Chill. Stir in the half-and-half. Serve over a glass half-full of ice.

SLOW AND STEADY

True friendship is a plant of slow growth,
and must undergo and withstand
the shocks of adversity before it
is entitled to the appellation.

—GEORGE WASHINGTON

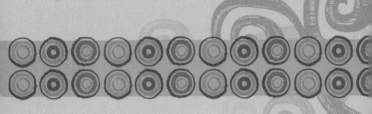

GiFT FROM ABOVE

Every good and perfect gift is from above,
coming down from the Father of the
heavenly lights, who does not change
like shifting shadows.

—JAMES 1:17 NIV

THE SHORTEST ROAD

To a friend's house, the road is never long.

—UNKNOWN

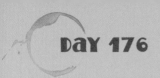

DaY 176

UNDER ALL CONDITIONS. . .

When you have no helpers, see your
helpers in God. When you have many
helpers, see God in all your helpers.
When you have nothing but God, see all
in God. When you have everything, see God
in everything. Under all conditions,
stay thy heart only on the Lord.

—Charles H. Spurgeon

SCHOOLS OF WISDOM

The first coffeehouses in Constantinople
around 1554 were called *Kahveh kanes*
(schools of the wise) because they
were the luxurious meeting places
of men of arts and literature.

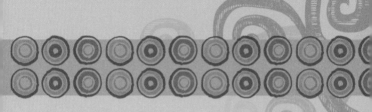

THREE METHODS

By three methods we may learn wisdom:
First, by reflection, which is noblest;
second, by imitation, which is easiest;
and third, by experience, which is the bitterest.

—CONFUCIUS

Faith

Faith sees the invisible, believes the
unbelievable, and receives the impossible.

—Corrie ten Boom

Recycle

Recycle those coffee cans. They make
great storage containers, or use them to
ship cookies and candy gifts during the
holidays. Cover the outside with
self-sticking shelving paper or wrapping paper.

Faith Is. . .

Now faith is being sure of what we hope for and certain of what we do not see.

—Hebrews 11:1 NIV

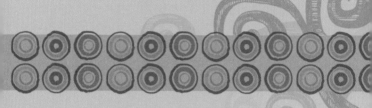

No Explanation Necessary

To one who has faith, no explanation is
necessary. To one without faith,
no explanation is possible.

—Thomas Aquinas

COFFEE PUNCH

2 quarts strong brewed coffee, chilled
2 cups milk
½ cup sugar
1 tablespoon vanilla
2 quarts vanilla ice cream, softened
2 cups whipping cream, whipped
Nutmeg

Blend together coffee, milk, sugar, and vanilla. Chill. Place vanilla ice cream in large punch bowl. Pour coffee mixture over top of ice cream and stir gently to combine. Top punch bowl or individual cups with whipped cream and a dusting of nutmeg.

DANCE OF HOPE

He that lives in hope dances without music.

—GEORGE HERBERT

GREAT COMPROMISE

Making coffee has become the great compromise of the decade. It's the only thing "real" men do that doesn't seem to threaten their masculinity. To women, it's on the same domestic entry level as putting the spring back into the toilet-tissue holder or taking a chicken out of the freezer to thaw.

—Erma Bombeck

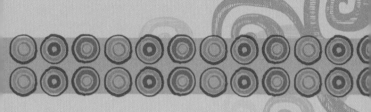

GO THROUGH

The best way out is always through.

—ROBERT FROST

PROBLEMS

No problem is so big or so complicated that it can't be run away from!

—LINUS VAN PELT
(CHARLES SCHULZ'S *PEANUTS*)

DAY 188

THIS IS THE WAY

Whether you turn to the right or to the left, your ears will hear a voice behind you, saying, "This is the way; walk in it."

—ISAIAH 30:21 NIV

LOVE THE LEADER

Faith never knows where it is being led,
but it loves and knows the One who is leading.

—OSWALD CHAMBERS

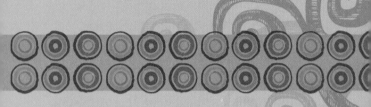

DOORS OF WISDOM

The doors of wisdom are never shut.

—BENJAMIN FRANKLIN

THE PRESIDENTIAL CUP

I never drink coffee at lunch.
I find it keeps me awake for the afternoon.

—RONALD REAGAN

CHOCOLATE-
DIPPED SPOONS

Melt chocolate chips (2 ounces will do about
8 spoons) over low heat until smooth.
Dip plastic spoons up to the start of the
handle, allowing a good bit of chocolate
to pool in the bowl. You can sprinkle with
crushed candy while wet, then let dry. Use
spoons for stirring your coffee.

WORK AND PRAY

Work as if everything depended on you and
pray as if everything depended on God.

—DWIGHT L. MOODY

DaY 194

Seek Glory

To those who by persistence in doing good seek glory, honor and immortality, he will give eternal life.

—Romans 2:7 NIV

TRUE HAPPINESS

True happiness consists not in the multitude of friends, but in their worth and choice.

—SAMUEL JOHNSTON

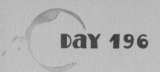

CREATE THE FUTURE

There is nothing like a dream
to create the future.

—VICTOR HUGO

SURPRISED BY CHANGE

Time changes everything except
something within us which is
always surprised by change.

—THOMAS HARDY

ICED BERRY BURST

1 (10 ounce) package frozen raspberries
½ cup sugar
½ cup water
10 cups cold, brewed coffee
1 pint half-and-half
Chipped ice
1 cup whipped topping
Mint sprigs
Whole raspberries

Place frozen raspberries, sugar, and water in a blender and mix until smooth. Strain mixture into a large mixing bowl, eliminating seeds. Add coffee and half-and-half and blend well. Fill chilled glasses half-full with chipped ice and pour berry mixture over ice. Garnish with whipped topping, mint sprigs, and whole raspberries.

—MARY & MARTHA

THE MEASURE OF LIFE

I have measured out my life
with coffee spoons.

—T. S. ELIOT

YOU CAN

Do all the good you can, by all the means you can, in all the ways you can, in all the places you can, at all the times you can, to all the people you can, as long as ever you can.

—CHARLES WESLEY

A GOOD MEASURE

*Give, and it will be given to you.
A good measure, pressed down, shaken
together and running over, will be poured
into your lap. For with the measure you use,
it will be measured to you.*

—LUKE 6:38 NIV

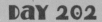

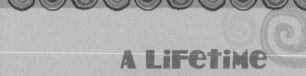

A LiFetime oF Happiness

The activity of happiness must occupy
an entire lifetime; for one swallow
does not a summer make.

—ARISTOTLE

COURAGE IS CONTAGIOUS

Courage is contagious. When a brave
man takes a stand, the spines
of others are stiffened.

—BILLY GRAHAM

CHARACTER EXHIBITED

Character is not made in a crisis;
it is only exhibited.

—ROBERT FREEMAN

THE HUMAN HEART

Actually, this seems to be the basic need of the human heart in nearly every great crisis—a good hot cup of coffee.

—ALEXANDER KING

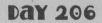

DAY 206

sweetness

Draw the honey out of the comb of Scripture,
and live on its sweetness.

—Charles H. Spurgeon

OUR DAILY BURDENS

Praise be to the Lord, to God our Savior,
who daily bears our burdens.

—Psalm 68:19 NIV

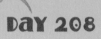

COCONUT COFFEE

1 whole coconut
2 cups milk
4 cups strong brewed coffee
1 tablespoon sugar

Make 2 holes in coconut and pour liquid out into a saucepan. Bake coconut at 300 degrees for 30 minutes. Open coconut and remove meat. Grate the meat and add it to the liquid in the saucepan. Add milk and heat over low until creamy. Strain out meat and toast it under a broiler. Add coffee and sugar to milk mixture. Pour into mugs garnished with toasted coconut.

HAPPY AFFECTIONS

The happiest moments my heart knows
are those in which it is pouring forth its
affections to a few esteemed characters.

—THOMAS JEFFERSON

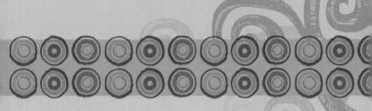

THE STREAM OF LIFE

Talent develops itself in solitude;
character in the stream of life.

—Johann Wolfgang von Goethe

OUT OF SORTS?

When late morning rolls around and you're
feeling a bit out of sorts, don't worry;
you're probably just a little eleven o'clockish.

—*WINNIE THE POOH*, BY A. A. MILNE

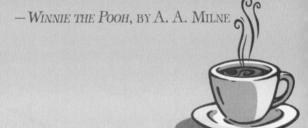

A MORNING PERSON

All the coffee in Columbia won't
make me a morning person.

—UNKNOWN

MY SOUL WAITS

*I wait for the LORD, my soul waits,
and in his word I put my hope. My soul
waits for the Lord more than watchmen
wait for the morning.*

—PSALM 130:5-6 NIV

Chocolate Coffee Dessert

Graham cracker squares (not crumbs)
2 cups whipping cream
½ cup powdered sugar
4 tablespoons chocolate syrup
1 tablespoon instant coffee granules
Chocolate garnish

Place a layer of graham crackers in 9x9-inch baking pan. Whip cream; add powdered sugar, chocolate syrup, and coffee. Place one-third of mixture on crackers. Repeat with another layer of crackers and second one-third of mixture; top with a third layer of crackers and last one-third of mixture. Garnish with chocolate.

Have Fun

People rarely succeed unless they
have fun in what they are doing.

—DALE CARNEGIE

WORKING TOGETHER

Coming together is the beginning;
keeping together is progress;
working together is success.

—HENRY FORD

A CUP OF JOE

During World War II, American servicemen, or G.I. Joes, were known to be excessive coffee drinkers. It is possible that the soldiers and those who served them coined the expression "cup of joe."

DAY 218

TO SERVE

Each one should use whatever gift he has received to serve others, faithfully administering God's grace in its various forms.

—1 PETER 4:10 NIV

CULTIVATE THE BEST

When we seek to discover the best in others,
we somehow bring out the best in ourselves.

—WILLIAM ARTHUR WARD

Disconnect

Make a pot of coffee and "disconnect" from the world. Turn off your cell phone, let the answering machine take care of your home phone calls, turn off the TV, and savor the silence. A little peace and quiet will rejuvenate your soul.

—MARY & MARTHA

A FRIEND'S HOUSE

Go often to the house of thy friend,
for weeds choke the unused path.

—RALPH WALDO EMERSON

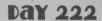

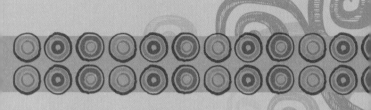

THE STORY OF MY LIFE

My friends have made the story of my life.
In a thousand ways they have turned my
limitations into beautiful privileges,
and enabled me to walk serene and happy
in the shadow cast by my deprivation.

—HELEN KELLER

A JUDICIOUS FRIEND

A judicious friend, into whose heart we may pour out our souls, and tell our corruptions as well as our comforts, is a very great privilege.

—GEORGE WHITEFIELD

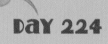

ANoTHER DaY

You are ushering in another day
Untouched and freshly new
So here I come to ask You, God,
If You'll renew me, too.
Forgive the many errors
That I made yesterday
And let me try again, dear God,
To walk closer in Thy way.

—HELEN STEINER RICE

An Earned Rest

Each morning sees some task begun,
each evening sees it close;
something attempted, something done,
has earned a night's repose.

—Henry Wadsworth Longfellow

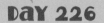

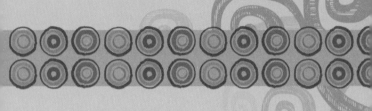

COFFee Float

2 teaspoons sugar
2½ cups hot, strong brewed coffee
⅔ cup cream
4 scoops coffee-flavored ice cream
1 large bottle cola

Add sugar to coffee and refrigerate. When chilled, add cream to coffee. Fill 4 glasses half-full, then add a scoop of ice cream to each glass. Top off each glass with cola.

GET IT RIGHT

If this is coffee, please bring me some tea;
but if this is tea, please bring me some coffee.

—ABRAHAM LINCOLN

A GOOD MEASURE

Give, and it will be given to you. A good measure, pressed down, shaken together and running over, will be poured into your lap.

—LUKE 6:38 NIV

THE STUFF OF LIFE

Dost thou love life? Then do not squander time, for that is the stuff life is made of.

—BENJAMIN FRANKLIN

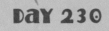

SUNSHINE

Love comforteth like sunshine after rain.

—WILLIAM SHAKESPEARE

KNOWLEDGE APPLIED

Wisdom is knowledge applied. Head knowledge is useless on the battlefield. Knowledge stamped on the heart makes one wise.

—BETH MOORE

LOOK TO THIS DAY

Look to this day. . .for yesterday is but a
dream, and tomorrow is only a vision. . .
but today well-lived makes every yesterday
a dream of happiness and every tomorrow a
vision of hope.

—UNKNOWN

SOMETHING TO LIVE FOR

Without friends no one would choose to live,
though he had all other goods.

—Augustine

DAY 234

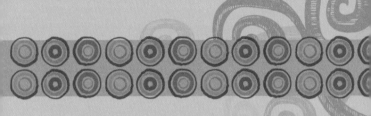

SOUTHERN COFFEE

Well, they're Southern people, and if they
know you are working at home they think
nothing of walking right in for coffee. But they
wouldn't dream of interrupting you at golf.

—HARPER LEE

TOO MANY BLESSINGS

Dear heavenly Father, thank You for the gift of friendship. In it we find love, laughter, comfort—too many blessings to name. Please help us to remember that although we don't always see eye to eye with our friends, they help us to broaden our horizons and see things from a new perspective. Amen.

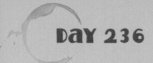

LOVE AND CHOCOLATE

All I really need is love, but a little chocolate
now and then doesn't hurt!

—LUCY VAN PELT
(CHARLES SCHULTZ'S *PEANUTS*)

FAMILY GATHERING

Gather your family together once
a week for devotions and (coffee).
Read through a family-friendly devotional
book or study a passage from the Bible.
End with prayer and a sweet treat!

—MARY & MARTHA

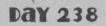

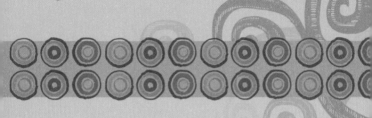

MEMORY OF THE TABLE

Ponder well on this point: The pleasant hours of our life are all connected by a more or less tangible link with some memory of the table.

—CHARLES PIERRE MONSELET

Long Live Love

Brief is life, but love is long.

—Alfred Lord Tennyson

EUROPEAN-STYLE COFFEE

2 egg whites
½ teaspoon vanilla
2 cups strong brewed coffee
¼ cup half-and-half

Beat egg whites until peaks start to form. Add vanilla and beat to stiff peaks. Divide into four coffee mugs. Pour coffee over egg whites and top off with half-and-half.

WORLD TRAVELER

A man travels the world over in search of
what he needs and returns home to find it.

—GEORGE MOORE

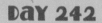

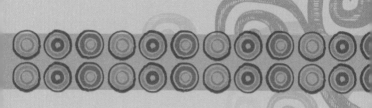

WITH THE ONES
YOU LOVE

Can miles truly separate you from friends...?
If you want to be with someone you love,
aren't you already there?

—RICHARD BACH

THE MORNING COFFEE

Without my morning coffee I'm just like a
dried up piece of roast goat.

—JOHANN SEBASTIAN BACH,
THE COFFEE CANTATA

EXCEPTIONS

The young man knows the rules,
but the old man knows the exceptions.

—OLIVER WENDELL HOLMES

THE MANY GOOD THINGS

*I will tell of the kindnesses of the LORD,
the deeds for which he is to be praised,
according to all the LORD has done for us—
yes, the many good things he has done.*

—ISAIAH 63:7 NIV

WEB OF LIFE

The web of our life is of a mingled yarn,
good and ill together.

—WILLIAM SHAKESPEARE

Mind Power

The powers of a man's mind
are directly proportional to the
quantity of coffee he drank.

—SIR JAMES MACKINTOSH

OUR BaSiC NeeD

Basically the only thing we need
is a hand that rests on our own, that wishes
it well, that sometimes guides us.

—HECTOR BIANCIOTTI

THE POWER OF TWO

Two are better than one; because they have a good reward for their labour. For if they fall, the one will lift up his fellow: but woe to him that is alone when he falleth; for he hath not another to help him up.

—ECCLESIASTES 4:9–10 KJV

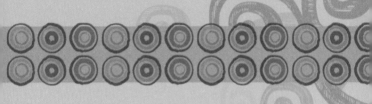

FRIENDS ARE GOLD

My friends are my estate. Forgive me then
the avarice to hoard them. They tell me those
who were poor early have different views of
gold. I don't know how that is. God is not so
wary as we, else He would give us no friends,
lest we forget Him.

—EMILY DICKINSON

Raspberry-Truffle Latte

6 ounces hot, brewed coffee
2 tablespoons chocolate syrup
2 tablespoons raspberry syrup
½ cup chocolate ice cream
Whipped topping
Grated chocolate
Fresh raspberries

Mix coffee and flavored syrups in mug. Spoon ice cream into coffee mixture. Add whipped topping, grated chocolate, and fresh raspberries as desired.

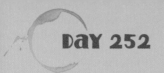

WISDOM OF THE HEART

There is a wisdom of the head,
and a wisdom of the heart.

—CHARLES DICKENS

WELL AGED

Grow old along with me, the best is yet to be.

—ROBERT BROWNING

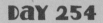

DAY 254

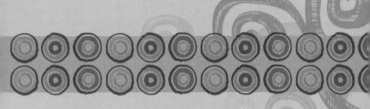

AGELESS WISDOM

Is not wisdom found among the aged?
Does not long life bring understanding?

—JOB 12:12 NIV

SIP OF PLEASURE

Last comes the beverage of the Orient shore, Mocha, far off, the fragrant berries bore. Taste the dark fluid with a dainty lip, digestion waits on pleasure as you sip.

—POPE LEO XII

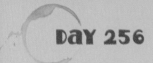

A LAUGH A DAY

The most wasted of all days
is one without laughter.

—E.E. CUMMINGS

BRING CHEER

The best way to cheer yourself up
is to try to cheer someone else up.

—MARK TWAIN

Be Joyful

Make the conscious choice to be joyful.
You'll be delighted at what a change
this simple but powerful choice
will make in your life!

—Mary & Martha

NUMBER OUR DAYS

*So teach us to number our days,
that we may apply our hearts unto wisdom.*

—PSALM 90:12 KJV

THE REAL THINGS

It is the sweet, simple things of life
which are the real ones after all.

—LAURA INGALLS WILDER

PLATFORMS IN LIFE

All our difficulties are only platforms for the manifestation of His grace, power, and love.

—HUDSON TAYLOR

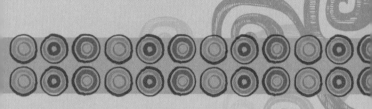

LIFE IN YOUR YEARS

Live decently, fearlessly, joyously and
don't forget that in the long run it is not
the years in your life but the life
in your years that counts!

—ADLAI STEVENSON

TIME TO BREW

Forever: Time it takes to brew the
first pot of coffee in the morning.

—Unknown

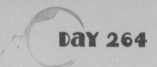

Love with Actions

Let us not love with words or tongue but with actions and in truth.

—1 John 3:18 niv

TAKE A TIME-OUT

If you are overworked and overstressed,
take a time-out and do absolutely nothing
all by yourself. Savor this time and let
the Lord speak to your heart.

—MARY & MARTHA

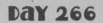

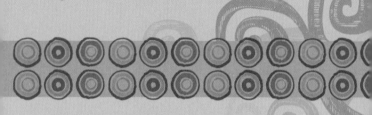

Persevere

By perseverance the snail reached the ark.

—Charles H. Spurgeon

AWASH IN LAUGHS

What soap is to the body,
laughter is to the soul.

—Yiddish Proverb

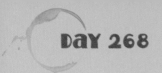

GOOD MEDICINE

A merry heart doeth good like a medicine:
but a broken spirit drieth the bones.

—PROVERBS 17:22 KJV

A FIRST FRIEND

Some people may still have their first dollar,
but the man who is really wealthy is the
fellow who still has his first friend.

—UKNOWN

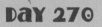

Instant Cappuccino

⅔ cup instant coffee
1 cup powdered sugar
1 cup powdered chocolate milk mix
½ cup sugar
½ teaspoon cinnamon
½ teaspoon nutmeg
Boiling water

Create a fine texture to the instant coffee by putting it through a blender or coffee grinder. Combine all dry ingredients and mix well. Use 1 to 2 heaping tablespoons per cup of boiling water. Store drink mix in an airtight container.

—MARY & MARTHA

THE IDEAL LIFE

Good friends, good books, and a sleepy
conscience: this is the ideal life.

—MARK TWAIN

WITHOUT CAFFEINE

Sleep is a symptom of caffeine deprivation.

—UNKNOWN

MASTERPIECE

A friend may well be reckoned
the masterpiece of nature.

—Ralph Waldo Emerson

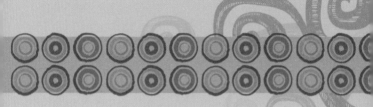

It Takes Two

It's so much more friendly with two.

—Piglet, by A. A. Milne

COFFEE FOR TWO

Invite a friend over for coffee or tea. You'll find that the conversation and company will lift your spirit and rejuvenate your soul.

—MARY & MARTHA

NEIGHBORLY DUTY

My duty towards my neighbor is to love him as myself, and to do unto all men as I would they should do unto me.

—BOOK OF COMMON PRAYER

QUIETNESS AND PEACE

O God, make us children of quietness
and children of peace.

—CLEMENT OF ROME

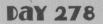

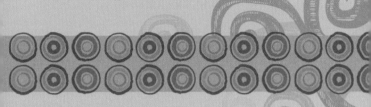

COFFEE IS. . .

Coffee is often better known as break fluid.

THE NATURE STATION

I love to think of nature as an
unlimited broadcasting station through
which God speaks to us every hour,
if we will only tune in.

—GEORGE WASHINGTON CARVER

Don't Worry

Therefore I tell you, do not worry about your life, what you will eat or drink.

—Matthew 6:25 NIV

Not Older—Newer

We turn, not older with years,
but newer every day.

—Emily Dickinson

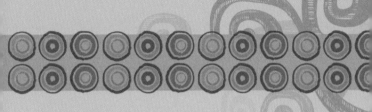

PUMPKIN-SPICE Latte

1 shot (1 to 1.5 ounce) brewed espresso
2 tablespoons canned pumpkin puree
1 teaspoon vanilla
2 tablespoons sugar
¼ teaspoon pumpkin pie spice
1 cup milk

While preparing espresso, whisk together
pumpkin, vanilla, sugar, pumpkin pie spice,
and milk in a small saucepan over medium
heat. Stir constantly until hot and frothy.
Do not boil. Pour espresso into a mug
and top off with pumpkin mixture.

NeVeR tOO WeaK

Don't laugh at the coffee.
Someday you, too, may be old and weak.

—Unknown

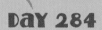

SUFFICIENT GRACE

Soar back through all your own experiences. Think of how the Lord has led you in the wilderness and has fed and clothed you every day. How God has borne with your ill manners, and put up with all your murmurings and all your longings after the "sensual pleasures of Egypt!" Think of how the Lord's grace has been sufficient for you in all your troubles.

—Charles H. Spurgeon

peace

A heart at peace gives life to the body.

—Proverbs 14:30 NIV

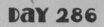

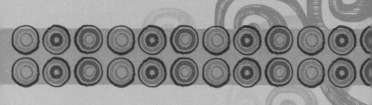

ART OF BEING WISE

The art of being wise is the
art of knowing what to overlook.

—WILLIAM JAMES

TOMORROW

Don't worry about the world coming to an end today. It's already tomorrow in Australia.

—CHARLES SCHULZ

A WISE OLD BIRD

A wise old owl sat on an oak,
The more he saw the less he spoke;
The less he spoke the more he heard;
Why aren't we like that wise old bird?

—Edward Hersey Richards

Listen Up!

What people really need
is a good listening to.

—MARY LOU CASEY

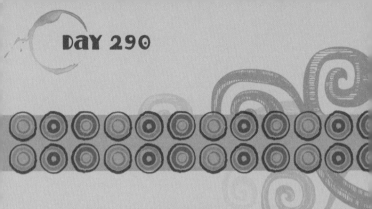

BLACK

Do I like my coffee black?
There are other colors?

—UNKNOWN

IF I can. . .

If I can do some good today,
If I can serve along life's way,
If I can something helpful say,
Lord, show me how.
If I can right a human wrong,
If I can help to make one strong,
If I can cheer with smile or song,
Lord, show me how.
If I can aid one in distress,
If I can make a burden less,
If I can spread more happiness,
Lord, show me how.

—Grenville Kleiser

DAY 292
FIRESIDE MOCHA MIX

2 cups nondairy coffee creamer
1½ cups instant coffee mix
1½ cups hot cocoa mix
1½ cups sugar
1 teaspoon cinnamon
¼ teaspoon nutmeg

In a large bowl, combine all ingredients.
Store mixture in an airtight container.
To prepare 1 serving, stir 2 heaping
tablespoons of mix into 1 cup boiling water.
Yield: 40 prepared cups.

—MARY & MARTHA

Radiance

There are persons so radiant, so genial,
so kind, so pleasure-bearing, that you
instinctively feel in their presence that they
do you good, whose coming into a room is
like the bringing of a lamp there.

—HENRY WARD BEECHER

DAY 294

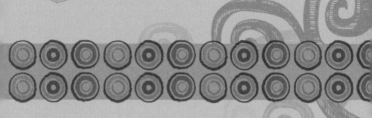

THINK ALOUD

A friend is a person with whom I may be sincere. Before him I may think aloud.

—RALPH WALDO EMERSON

PHILOSOPHERS

Coffee makes us severe, and grave,
and philosophical.

—JONATHAN SWIFT

Desperate Alternative

If ever in a desperate situation where a natural alternative is needed to fill the taste for coffee without the kick of caffeine, consider roasted chicory or dandelion root.

Be Still

*Be still before the Lord and
wait patiently for him.*

—Psalm 37:7 NIV

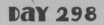

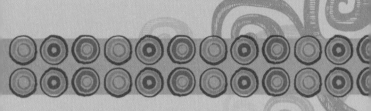

Live With Witnesses

Life without a friend is like
death without a witness.

—SPANISH PROVERB

CHAINED WITH FRIENDS

It is better to be in chains with friends,
than to be in a garden with strangers.

—PERSIAN PROVERB

A Severe Loss

The death of a friend is equivalent
to the loss of a limb.

—German Proverb

Mexican-style Coffee

2 cups water
¼ cup coarse coffee grounds
1 tablespoon brown sugar
1 cinnamon stick

Place all ingredients into a saucepan and heat to boiling. Simmer for about 5 minutes. Strain into mugs.

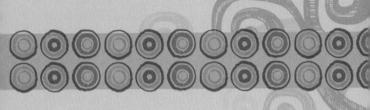

A HEART POURED OUT

A friend is one to whom one may pour
out all the contents of one's heart, chaff
and grain together, knowing that the
gentlest of hands will take and sift it,
keep what is worth keeping and with a
breath of kindness blow the rest away.

—Arabian Proverb

THE NEEDY FRIEND

A friend in need is a friend indeed.

—LATIN PROVERB

PLACE OF WARMTH

On days when warmth is the most important
need of the human heart, the kitchen is the
place you can find it.

—E. B. WHITE

OPEN MY EYES

Open my eyes, that I may see
Glimpses of truth thou hast for me;
Place in my hands the wonderful key
That shall unclasp and set me free.
Silently now I wait for thee,
Ready, my God, thy will to see;
Open my eyes, illumine me,
Spirit divine!

—CLARA H. SCOTT

ABIDE WITH ME

Abide with me from morn till eve,
For without Thee I cannot live;
Abide with me when night is nigh,
For without Thee I dare not die.

—JOHN KEBLE

StiMuLation

Good communication is just as
stimulating as black coffee,
and just as hard to sleep after.

—ANNE MORROW LINDBERGH

Quick to Listen

*Everyone should be quick to listen,
slow to speak and slow to become angry.*

—James 1:19 NIV

THE WORTH OF HUMOR

In conversation, humor is worth more than
wit and easiness more than knowledge.

—GEORGE HERBERT

Laughter Through Tears

My great hope is to laugh as much as I cry;
to get my work done and try to love
somebody and have the courage to
accept the love in return.

—Maya Angelou

HOW TO BUY LOVE

I believe that love cannot
be bought except with love.

—JOHN STEINBECK

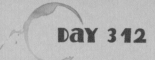

Black, Strong, and Sweet

Coffee should be black as hell,
strong as death, and sweet as love.

—Turkish Proverb

SAY NO

If you're overextended, learn to say no!
You'll be a happier person for it. . .and you'll
find that you enjoy having the freedom to
do something that isn't an obligation.

—MARY & MARTHA

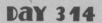

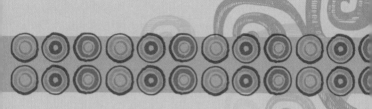

LAUGH IT THROUGH

If you can't make it better,
you can laugh at it.

—ERMA BOMBECK

HEAVEN LAUGHS

If you are not allowed to laugh in heaven,
I don't want to go there.

—MARTIN LUTHER

A Loveable
Sense of Humor

I love people who make me laugh. I honestly
think it's the thing I like most, to laugh.
It cures a multitude of ills. It's probably the
most important thing in a person.

—Audrey Hepburn

A SOCIAL BINDER

Over second and third cups flow matters of
high finance, high state, common gossip
and low comedy. [Coffee] is a social binder,
a warmer of tongues, a soberer of minds,
a stimulant of wit, a foiler of sleep if you
want it so. From roadside mugs to the classic
demitasse, it is the perfect democrat.

—UNKNOWN

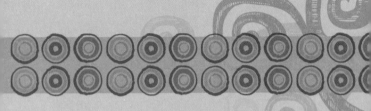

JOY AND SORROW

Friends are needed for both joy and sorrow.

—YIDDISH PROVERB

WHATEVER YOU DO

So whether you eat or drink or whatever you do, do it all for the glory of God.

—1 Corinthians 10:31 NIV

DAY 320

MEET & GREET

If you're the first person to arrive home in
the afternoon, make an effort to greet your
family members at the door with a smile!
This simple gesture will make them feel
loved and appreciated.

—MARY & MARTHA

sweeten the pain

So long as you can sweeten another's pain,
life is not in vain.

—HELEN KELLER

A FRIEND UNCHANGEABLE

A true friend unbosoms freely, advises justly,
assists readily, adventures boldly,
takes all patiently, defends courageously,
and continues a friend unchangeably.

—WILLIAM PENN

SILENCE IS FRIENDLY

In the end, we will remember
not the words of our enemies,
but the silence of our friends.

—MARTIN LUTHER KING JR.

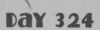

NOGGED COFFEE

½ cup cream
1 tablespoon sugar
1 egg yolk
1 cup hot, brewed coffee
Nutmeg

In a saucepan, heat cream over low heat. Beat sugar into egg yolk, then whisk into cream. Heat until it is just about to boil. Pour coffee into 2 mugs and top with cream mixture. Garnish with a sprinkle of nutmeg.

Real Conversations

Silences make the real conversations
between friends. Not the saying but the
never needing to say is what counts.

—Margaret Lee Runbeck

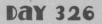

concentrations

A dark roast coffee has less caffeine
than a medium roast. And a fine ground
bean will produce a stronger brew than
a coarse ground bean.

APPRECIATION THROUGH EXPERIENCE

The more one does and sees and feels, the more one is able to do, and the more genuine may be one's appreciation of fundamental things like home, and love, and understanding companionship.

—AMELIA EARHART

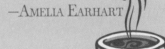

PRESS ON

*I press toward the mark for the prize of the
high calling of God in Christ Jesus.*

—Philippians 3:14 KJV

TAKE THE RISK

Only those who will risk going too far can
possibly find out how far one can go.

—T. S. ELIOT

DAY 330

COUNT YOUR BLESSINGS

Do you find that you spend too much time
worrying about what you just have to get
done? Intentionally redirect your thoughts
toward gratitude. What are you most thankful
for? Your health? A loving family?
A great career? You'll quickly forget about
your worries when you see how richly
the Lord has blessed you.

—MARY & MARTHA

MAGIC MIRRORS

Family faces are magic mirrors.
Looking at people who belong to us,
we see the past, present and future.
We make discoveries about ourselves.

—GAIL LUMET BUCKLEY

DaY 332

COFFEE anD MEN

Coffee leads men to trifle away their time, scald their chops, and spend their money, all for a little base, black, thick, nasty, bitter, stinking nauseous puddle water.

—THE WOMEN'S PETITION AGAINST COFFEE, 1674

SOMEONE TO COME HOME TO

One of the oldest human needs is having someone to wonder where you are when you don't come home at night.

—MARGARET MEAD

PRAYER FOR FAMILIES

God, give our households the same sweet
harmony I hear in the birds' songs.
Stabilize and strengthen our families.
Restore the sanctity of marriage.
Let parents demonstrate a respect and love
for each other that children may imitate.
Keep us from indulging our children,
confusing material excess with spiritual
necessity. Soothe the occasional ruffled
feathers, and teach us to live in
blessed concert. Amen.

—MARSHA MAURER

HOME IS WHERE THE HEART IS

Where we love is home. . .home that our feet
may leave, but not our hearts.

—OLIVER WENDELL HOLMES SR.

COMFORTS OF HOME

There is nothing like staying
at home for real comfort.

—JANE AUSTEN

HOME SWEET HOME

Every house where love abides
And friendship is a guest,
Is surely home, and home sweet home
For there the heart can rest.

—HENRY VAN DYKE

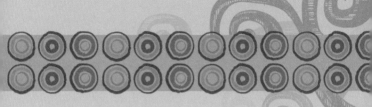

Thanksgiving

Give thanks to the LORD, for he is good.

—Psalm 136:1 NIV

THE SWEET SPOT

Home, the spot of earth supremely blest,
A dearer, sweeter spot than all the rest.

—ROBERT MONTGOMERY

Mocha Fudge

1 cup pecans, chopped
3 cups semisweet chocolate chips
1 (14 ounce) can sweetened condensed milk
2 tablespoons strong, brewed coffee, room temperature
1 teaspoon cinnamon
⅛ teaspoon salt
1 teaspoon vanilla

Line 8x8-inch pan with foil. Butter foil and set pan aside. Microwave pecans on high 4 minutes, stirring after each minute. In 2-quart microwave-safe bowl, mix chocolate, milk, coffee, cinnamon, and salt. Microwave on high 1½ minutes. Stir until smooth. Stir in pecans and vanilla. Cover and refrigerate until firm, about 2 hours. Remove from pan and cut into squares.

THE RICHEST

Chocolate, men, coffee:
some things are better rich.

—UNKNOWN

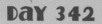

DAY 342

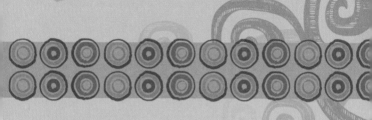

QUIET MY SOUL, LORD

Quiet my soul, Lord. Help me to lay my worries and stresses at Your feet and focus on enjoying time with my family. Remind me that it's okay to cut out the unnecessary tasks today and to leave some things for tomorrow. Amen.

—MARY & MARTHA

On Bended Knee

A lot of kneeling will keep
you in good standing.

—Unknown

THROUGH THE EYES OF COFFEE

Coffee, which makes the politician wise
And see through all things with
his half-shut eyes. . .

—ALEXANDER POPE

POiNT OF VIEW

You never really understand a person until
you consider things from his point of view—
until you climb inside of his skin and walk
around in it.

—ATTICUS FINCH IN *TO KILL A MOCKINGBIRD*,
BY HARPER LEE

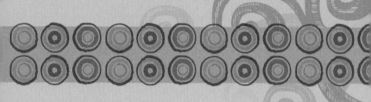

HOLIDAY STIRRER

Dip a candy cane into melted chocolate.
Let it dry. Then use the stick to
stir your evening coffee.

Be at Peace

Peace I leave with you; my peace I give you.
I do not give to you as the world gives.
Do not let your hearts be troubled.

—John 14:27 NIV

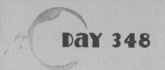

contentment

The utmost we can hope for
in this life is contentment.

—JOSEPH ADDISON

DOING NOTHING

Don't underestimate the value of Doing Nothing, of just going along, listening to all the things you can't hear, and not bothering.

— *WINNIE THE POOH*, BY A. A. MILNE

SHORTCUT ESPRESSO BISCOTTI

1 chocolate cake mix
1 cup flour
2 tablespoons espresso powder
½ cup butter, melted
2 eggs
1 teaspoon vanilla
½ cup pecans, chopped

Preheat oven to 350 degrees. Combine all ingredients except pecans in bowl. Mix well; add pecans. Divide dough in half and shape into foot-long flattened logs; place logs on greased baking sheet. Bake 30 to 35 minutes, until lightly browned. Cool on baking sheets for about 15 minutes, then cut logs into ½-inch slices. Return slices to pan and bake an additional 10 minutes and then cool completely.

SERENITY PRAYER

God, grant me. . .
Serenity to accept the things I cannot change,
Courage to change the things I can, and
Wisdom to know the difference.

—REINHOLD NIEBUHR

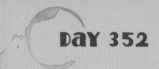

REVOLUTIONARY VISION

Look at everything as though you were seeing it either for the first or last time.

—BETTY SMITH,
A TREE GROWS IN BROOKLYN

No Nonsense

I would rather suffer with coffee
than be senseless.

—Napoléon Bonaparte

Blessed to Give

The Lord Jesus himself said:
"It is more blessed to give than to receive."

—Acts 20:35 NIV

COFFEE MEETS EGGNOG

When around the holidays you have eggnog in the refrigerator, try sweetening up your cup of coffee with a bit of the eggnog.

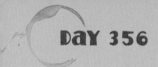

CHILDLiKe

It is good to be children sometimes, and
never better than at Christmas, when its
mighty Founder was a child Himself.

—CHARLES DICKENS

A WISE MAN

He is a wise man who does not grieve
for the things which he has not,
but rejoices for those which he has.

—EPICTETUS

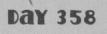

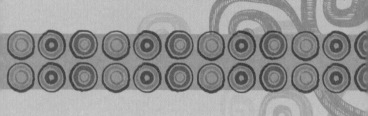

JOY

A joy that is shared is a joy made double.

—ENGLISH PROVERB

JOY RETURNS

Somehow, not only for Christmas,
But all the long year through,
The joy that you give to others,
Is the joy that comes back to you.

—JOHN GREENLEAF WHITTIER

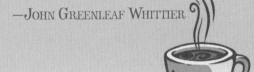

NO LONGER COMMON

We would take something old and tired
and common—coffee—and weave a sense
of romance and community around it.
We would rediscover the mystique and
charm that had swirled around
coffee throughout the centuries.

—HOWARD SCHUTZ, CEO OF STARBUCKS, 1997

CHRISTMAS MORNING COFFEE

1 pot (10 cups) brewed coffee
⅓ cup water
½ cup sugar
¼ cup unsweetened cocoa
¼ teaspoon cinnamon
1 pinch grated nutmeg
Sweetened whipped topping (optional)

Prepare coffee. While coffee is brewing, heat water
to a low boil in a large saucepan. Stir in sugar, cocoa,
cinnamon, and nutmeg. Bring back to a low boil for
1 minute, stirring occasionally. Combine coffee with
cocoa/spice mixture in saucepan. To serve, pour into
mugs and top with sweetened whipped topping if
desired. Yield: 10 servings.

—MARY & MARTHA

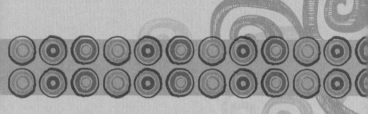

TRIED AND TRUE

O the world is wide and the world is grand,
And there's little or nothing new,
But its sweetest thing is the grip of the hand
Of the friend who's tried and true.

—UNKNOWN

we thank thee

For all the blessings of the year,
For all the friends we hold so dear,
For peace on earth, both far and near,
We thank thee, Lord.
For life and health, those common things,
Which every day and hour brings,
For home, where our affection clings,
We thank thee, Lord.
For love of thine, which never tires,
Which all our better thought inspires,
And warms our lives with heavenly fires
We thank thee, Lord.

—ALBERT H. HUTCHINSON

№ QUITTING

I'd stop drinking coffee, but I'm no quitter.

—UNKNOWN

GIVE HOPE A CHANCE

Beginnings are always scary,
endings are usually sad, but it's the
middle that counts. You just have
to give hope a chance to float up.

—STEVEN ROGERS

Notes